Bugs Book For Kids: It's a Bugs World

Speedy Publishing LLC
40 E. Main St. #1156
Newark, DE 19711

www.speedypublishing.com

9781681275901
First Printed January 19, 2015

Bugs Facts:

A bug is a certain type of insect. Some examples you might be familiar with are the boxelder bug, milkweed bug, assassin bug, and stink bug.

Bugs Facts:

Beetles account for one quarter of all known species of plants and animals. There are more kinds of beetles than all plants.

Bugs Facts:

Not all insects drown in water. In fact, quite a few live there for at least part of their lives. Insects breathe through holes in the sides of their bodies.

Bugs Facts:

Ants leave trails and communicate with each other using pheromones as chemical signals.

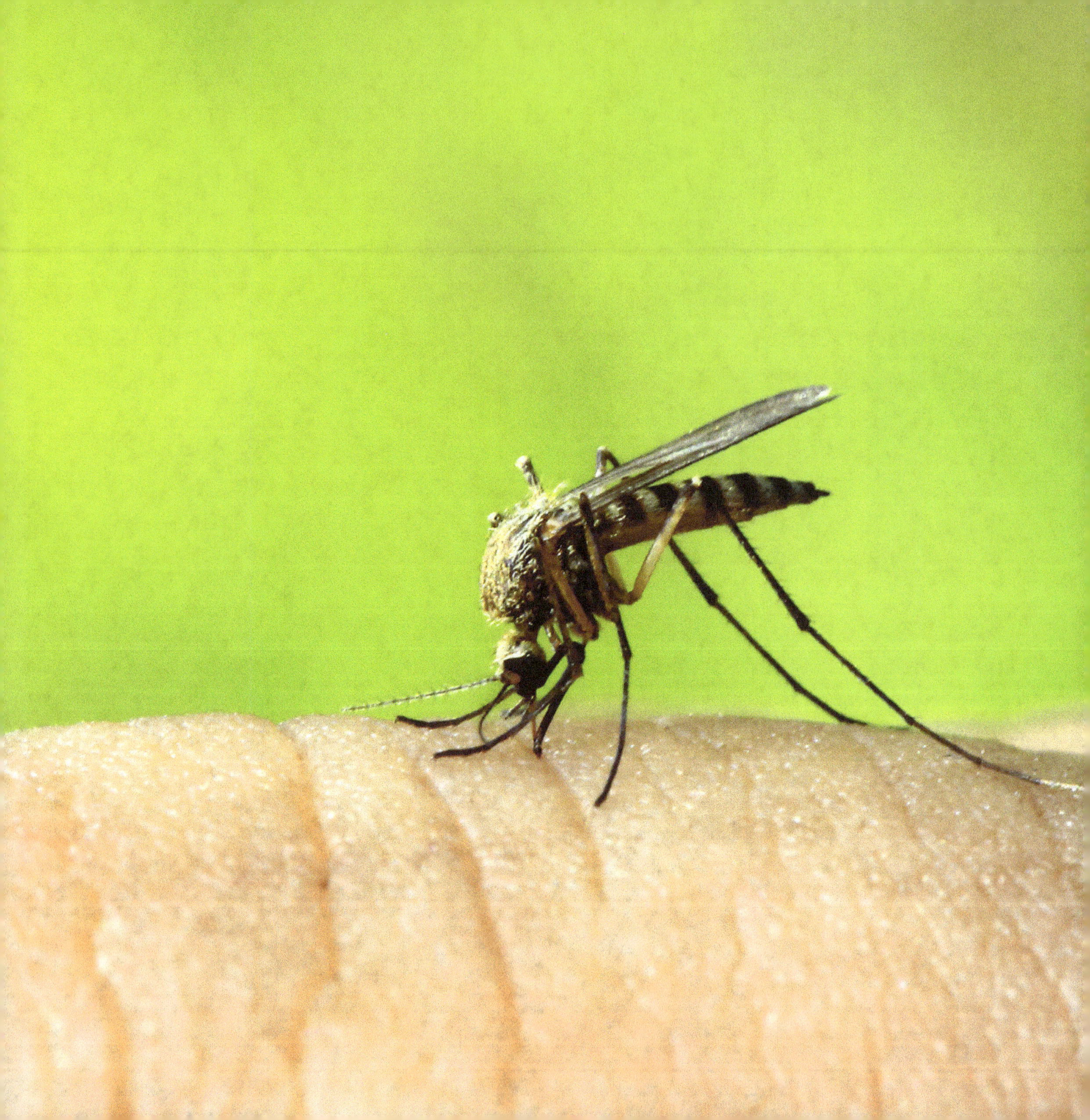

Bugs Facts:

The life cycle of a mosquito features four stages, egg, larva, pupa and adult. Female mosquitoes drink blood in order to obtain nutrients needed to produce eggs.

Bugs Facts:

Bees, termites and ants live in well organized social colonies.

Bugs Facts:

Some insects, such as gerridae (water striders), are able to walk on the surface of water.

Bugs Facts:

The queen of a certain termite species can lay 40,000 eggs per day.

Bugs Facts:

Cockroaches can eat just about anything, and can survive without food for long periods of time.

Bugs Facts:

Ants can lift and carry more than fifty times their own weight.

Bugs Facts:

Insects date back to over 300 million years!

Bugs Facts:

Dragonflies keep their wings spread out when at rest. Most Damselflies hold their wings together above their backs when they rest. They both eat mosquitoes and are good to have around!

Bugs Facts:

Mother Dung Beetles tenderly care for their young by cleaning away toxic molds and fungi off the dung balls where her larva lives and feasts.

Bugs Facts:

Lightningbugs or Fireflies are not true bugs or flies. They are actually beetles.

www.ingramcontent.com/pod-product-compliance
Lightning Source LLC
LaVergne TN
LVHW060830170826
845678LV00010B/1939

9798869457318